THE 72 HOUR AUTHENTICATION OF THE CHRIST

Christ's Only Sign

THE 72 HOUR AUTHENTICATION OF THE CHRIST

Christ's Only Sign

KELLY DON FORD

ReadersMagnet, LLC

CONTENTS

THE 72 HOUR AUTHENTICATION OF THE CHRIST

Christ's Only Sign

KELLY DON FORD

*"This was the only sign Jesus gave that he was the Christ—
that he had to be in the tomb exactly 72 hours or else he was
not our Savior."*

— Ingram Christian Advance

CHAPTER 1

BIBLE WORD STUDIES

The Biblical quotes are taken from the King James Version (KJV). I realize that there are many translations out there. I am also aware of the many archaic words used in the KJV. It reads like Shakespeare to some people and is hard to comprehend but because others were brought up on it, they are more comfortable with it. There is a lot of disagreement and debate on which translations are the best or right. When I do in-depth studies covering a wide range of Scriptures, I tend to use the KJV because of its origin and connection to the Textus Receptus, as opposed to the Alexandrian Texts where corrupt versions most abound. If we continued in that vein, we would not finish the task at hand. To me, it is the most accurate to the original. I also chose the KJV because of the beauty, flow, and readability. With the verses throughout this text, there is no problem with accuracy.

I think this information is more critical now than ever before which results in this new book, based on Part 2 of my 1998 title "Ancient Signs of Deception". At that time, an awakening had begun and more have been written about this subject since. The results I have seen are still slightly off-center and I believe this treatise will guide us home.

At this point I feel I need to speak about the subject of word studies as it applies to the Bible. It would do well for all of us to study the Word of God more. II Timothy 2:15 "Study to show thyself approved of God, a workman that needeth not to be ashamed, rightly dividing the word of truth." (KJV) There are many Greek New Testament word-for-word text books that help tremendously as well as Hebrew and Chaldean for the Old Testament. There are two words I would like to look at in brief. The first one is found in the Old Testament in Exodus 20:13. The last word in that verse *ratsach* is often translated as kill when it means murder. A lot of the debates we hear and see about capital punishment could quickly be put to rest once the words kill and murder are defined. The second word is love. The Greeks had at least six words that are translated as love: 1) *agape*- unconditional, eternal, consistent; 2) *phileo*- fellowship, comradeship, friendship, bond; 3) *storge*- belonging as to a family; 4) *eros*- erotic, sexual, romantic; 5) *epithumia*- lovemaking; 6) *thelo*- desire, to wish. Most of the time, when used in context we can know what is meant when the word love is used. There is one example found in John 21: 15-17 that is an exception I would like to point out. If you read these passages in your own Bible, you will get a better comprehension of the application. When Jesus asks Peter the first time if he loves Him, He uses the word *agape*. When Peter answers him, he uses the word *phileo*. After denying Christ three times, Peter may not have wanted to commit to or feel worthy of loving as defined by *agape*. Jesus asks him the second time if he *agapes* Him and again Peter answers with the word *phileo*. The compassionate, understanding, and forgiving Jesus asks him the third time. But in this particular instance, he uses the word *phileo*. You see, deeper meanings are conveyed when we do word studies such as these that a casual reading might not reveal. Remember this when reading or studying your Bible. For those of you who know Jesus on a personal level, as needed, He loves us on our level, way, and time. Thank you, Jesus!

CHAPTER 2

HISTORY IN JESUS

Jesus is truly a historic figure. Christianity remains the world's largest religion in terms of population; however, Islam seems to be the fastest growing as of this printing. They, including Muslims, believe Jesus to an extent but stop much farther than other religions. They don't believe He has any part of what we term the Trinity or that He is equal with God, although they do accept Him as a prophet. Because of the Catholic Good Friday Miscount they can discount Him for the same reason. Most feel He missed or skipped the Cross and didn't die at all. The Bible is still the number one selling book, and it includes the New Testament, the revelation of Jesus Christ. History is actually *His story*. Even time itself is counted B.C. (before Christ) and A.D. (in the year of the Lord). Flavius Josephus, an early historian who was born in 37 A.D., wrote about Jesus: *Josephus Complete Works*, "Antiquities of the Jews", Chapter III. Christians or *Christ*-ians are followers of Christ, not just believers. Anyone can believe. James 2:19 states, "...the devils also believe and tremble." A non-active faith is no faith at all according to James

2:20-26 and Ephesians 2:8. Romans 10:17 preaches, "So then faith cometh by hearing, and hearing by the word of God." When we believe, we believe what Jesus says. His words and teachings become important to us as we read and study and live. In some Bibles, the words of Christ are printed in red ink for emphasis, easy recognition, and importance. When we believe, we don't just try. We do, or be, or will, or act.

John 20:30,31- "And many other signs truly did Jesus in the presence of his disciples, which are not written in this book: But these are written, that ye might believe that Jesus is the Christ, the Son of God; and that believing ye might have life in his name." John 21:25- "And there are also many other things which Jesus did, the which, if they should be written every one, I suppose that even the world itself could not contain the books that should be written." It would be ludicrous to say that Jesus didn't perform many wonderful and glorious signs, too numerous to count. Some of that day asked to see miraculous signs and wanted to test Jesus. The first scripture above tells the reason why the ones we have in the Bible were written down. Luke 24:44- "And he said unto them, These are the words which I spake unto you, while I was yet with you, that all things must be fulfilled, which were written in the law of Moses, and in the prophets, and in the psalms, concerning me."

CHAPTER 3

JESUS' ONLY SIGN

There was, however, one particular and significant sign that Jesus talked about that was like no other. He was to signify it by his Messiahship. The group he was addressing was a special group made up of Pharisees, and scribes, and Sadducees. It cannot be overstated that the law in reference to Judaism is crucial. These sects or parties or classes were responsible for the written law as well as its interpretation and application. They made rules and tried to adapt the law to their lives at that time. There were arguments and debates as to whether all law was to be written or some of it to be verbal and or told and handed down to subsequent generations. Regardless of their similarities and differences, most wanted to try to trick Jesus into nullifying any law so they could totally disregard Him. In other words, they were looking for an excuse to deny His rightful place. His words to them were absolute and emphatic. His words and actions had to stand the test of time, had to remain true, and had to fulfill prophecy and all righteousness. So, when they came to Him in Matthew 12:38 and in 16:1 to test Him and ask for a sign from heaven, He gave them the following statement in Matthew 12:39,40- "But he answered and said unto them, An evil and adulterous generation seeketh after a sign; and there shall no sign be given to it, but the sign of the prophet Jonas: For as Jonas was three days and three nights in the whale's belly; so shall the Son of Man be three days and three nights in the heart of the earth." Brothers and Sisters, this is CRITICAL, Indeed! And cannot be overstated. Because two of the world's religions are holding this against believing in Him attached to the one sign which I call the "Jesus Only Sign", that some still don't believe He fulfilled! And why? Well, it's directly tied to the largest religion, Christendom, which is still incorrectly preaching that Jesus only spent half the time he said he would be in the tomb in the heart of the earth. And that belief is none other than a Good Friday crucifixion and a Sunday sunrise, not a Sunday Son rise resurrection perpetuated by the Catholic church.

No sign shall be given to it except this one. Jesus meant what He said. Jesus carefully and methodically threw these words out in front of the keepers of the Law! If anyone was going to scrutinize and dot their i's and cross their t's it was these very groups He was addressing. This one sign has not been taken very seriously. The Jewish religion didn't believe He was the foretold Messiah anyway so it makes little difference to them that Christendom believes in a Good Friday crucifixion and a sunrise resurrection Sunday morning. The Old Testament as well as the Old Law was given to them in order to bring them to Christ but it failed in that part of its mission - sad in many ways.

We are currently being deceived. Jesus made no mention in this context that He was talking about only a part of three days. On the contrary, if it was important to Him, why shouldn't it be that important to us today? Who will listen? Who will hear? Who will understand? Has the past two thousand years obscured so obvious a truth? A lot was lost in those first critical 72 hours. Whether a crime, tragedy, or disaster, the first 72 hours are between the solving of an event like this or it becoming just another Cold Case. We will examine each piece of Biblical so-called paradox to reveal its simple pattern and truth. My motto has always been: Truth is where you find it.

This quick but thorough study, I believe, will truly enlighten you and help you to better understand God and his plan for us in observing the most correct time for the assembling of the saints early upon the first day of the week. These examples abound in your own Bible. So let's get started. Put Satan back in his place and out of ours. Remember, we don't want to give him the time to exist or have the power to rule any particular day or night.

CHAPTER 4

THE BAD THE GOOD
AND THE UGLY

Most of us have heard the expression or acronym, TGIF. Thank God It's Friday has been a worker's weekly battle cry as far back as I can remember. What does Friday have over any other day? Of course, we should be thankful for every day the Lord has made (Psalms 118:24 -- "This is the day which the Lord hath made; we will rejoice and be glad in it.") Let us cherish and be delighted in every day that we are allowed to experience and enjoy. Fridays have particular significance for many in this world. The world seemingly looks forward to the glorious weekend ahead. Plans are made. Heart rates rise. Serious fun begins. Dates are set. Paychecks are handed out. Cash is set aside and made available. Credit and debit cards are readied. Even bitcoins are counted! For the most part, the weekend revolves totally around Saturday night, either going into or coming out of that primetime frame. We have movies and songs reflecting the Saturday night fever and night life that are still so prevalent in this day and age. Some look for that next Stimulus package, unemployment benefits and monthly Social Security and disabilities. Friends go out to be with friends. People meet new friends, look for physical excitement, natural intoxication, and more. Boys and girls meet. You can feel electricity in the air and neon lights show the broad way and a wide gate and many are there that go therein (Matt 7:13). Elixirs of all kind abound, from powders and liquids, to shots and pills. Smoke bellows and fills the air from vapes. The 357 MAG, the .38 Special caliber revolver, as well as the .22 LR & WMR pistols and a few others still fall into a loose category of what's commonly designated: Saturday Night Specials. The initials or acronym SNS is also used to bring attention to a wide range of commercial products. Grab for the gusto as long as you can. No one looks forward for the time to come down. Setup for Saturday, and Sunday becomes the chaser with rest, relaxation and excitement being the sought-after norm, and a blue Monday being the farthest from anyone's mind. The end day of their weekend is Sunday, a pitiful place to put the first day of the week. And if Satan has any more power on any day of the week, Saturday it is! Reservations are all filled up, even in emergency rooms and police stations.

For others, various kinds of preparations are being made. For the Jewish religion, from the beginning of time until the end of it, the Sabbath begins at sunset on the Friday evening of each week. There is minor debate as to when Sabbaths begin. However, most attend to the sunset definition except for "nightfall" and "a few minutes before sunset". Sunset is best defined as the moment the sun disappears completely over the horizon. However, since the margin of error is so small, any of these definitions do not affect the Critical 72 hour outcome. Some could even use 6 P.M. as the start, which we will use briefly but only the number of hours. Punctuation, capitalization, paragraphs, chapter headings, and verses were not part of the Old or New Testament scrolls. They were added during translation for ease of locating and reading. Sometimes Sabbath is capitalized and sometimes it's not. I chose to capitalize it in most instances. The evening/night period and the morning/day period has always been a complete 24 hour period. From Biblical times until now, each 24 hour day begins and ends at sunset, two 12 hour periods. See Gen 1: and John 11:9. For Christendom, who has bought into the civil/legal time of each day beginning at midnight, Sunday morning still has a first day of the week significance. Sunday is supposed to be the strongest day of the week. "The Son arose at sunrise" has quite a familiar ring. Still, many wonderful activities are planned. Though most church doors are closed tight during Saturday night.

Do we live today in an evil and adulterous generation? Look around. We seem to have a very exaggerated and provocative one. The divorce rate is at an all-time high. More now than ever before has sex been more popular and accepted in mainstream society. Popular talk shows just keep coming up with the more bizarre and weird to let us sit in on the everyday happenings and new normalcy. Exploitation abounds.

Where do our choices come from? Do we decide? Or do we follow like sheep to the slaughter? Do we want others to take the blame for our actions and our decisions? "It's not my fault" or "I didn't do it" or "You can't blame me for it" are all familiar phrases. There is way too much enabling going on. Do we trust the establishment too much, be it our overseers or peers? Can the Bible be our guide and example today? Have we trusted mainstream religions instead of reading and studying being responsible ourselves? We are bound by certain customs, to not rock the boat, to not ignore nor give heed to some obvious truths.

CHAPTER 5

FROM NIGHT TO DAY

Now, we all can figure this out on our own. Because of the precession of the equinoxes, days and nights are not perfectly equal in 12 hour segments. So with the sun as our guide, we would probably settle for evening beginning at sunset with daylight fading. The definition of the word "even" (Greek word "opsia" best definition = evening) is most important when determining when Joseph of Arimathea came for the body of Jesus. It solely reveals to ALL whether Jesus made it to the TOMB before or after the start of the Sabbath. At sunset is when the sun first disappears on the horizon. Evening follows. So, when Joseph first came, and it was even or evening, then the Sabbath had begun. No amount of backtracking would have ever helped to lay Him in the tomb by the start of the Sabbath. There were too many tasks -- from checking on Jesus to see if he was dead, to transporting everything to the Tomb, plus carefully wrapping the body, and rolling the heavy stone in place.

As each Sunday approaches especially at Easter time, many religious thoughts go through our minds. Each year, spring brings with it a newness of life and resurrection. New scenes of beauty with all its marvels fill our lives and our senses and replaces the cold harsh death of the winter season firmly behind us. Let our minds go back to the cross and envision what it means to us and our world. This is *His* story or maybe *history* would be a better word, because our time as we know it is counted B.C. and A.D. respectively. Christians have a new life as they die to their old selves and are resurrected to walk by faith and newness of life (II Cor. 5:7; Romans 6:4). Behold all things have become new (II Cor. 5:17). Now is the time to share these views and these experiences with others. Especially since a lot of us have more time on our hands with the still threatening Covid-19 pandemic. Let's open our minds and eyes and see truth as never before. Let's think of how tradition (Mark 7:13; Col. 2:8) and what the world, as well as Christendom, would have us think about this time of year versus what Jesus wants us to truly know by His own word in the Bible, yea by His own mouth the words that He spoke. Let's turn to Matthew 12:40 - "for as Jonas was three days and three nights in the whale's belly; so shall the Son of Man be three days and three nights in the heart of the earth." Let these red-letter words sink in. Any tradition which is in variance to this is to be shunned. Jesus uses the conjunction *and* twice. This joins the three days to the three nights making them inseparable. Verse 39 tells us that this will be the *only sign* given to an evil and adulterous generation. Very powerful! If Jesus is who

He says he is, this sign must come to pass. Jesus places the authenticity of his Messiahship, critical both then and especially now on this sign being fulfilled. Let's ask a few questions. First, how long are our days and nights? Well, for the record, both joined together are a total of 24 hours. Second, how long was a Jewish day and night? Going back to the book of Genesis, we find that the evening and the morning was one day. The Jewish day began with evening at, and for accounting sake only, 6 P.M., six hours before midnight and extended to the next day at 6 A.M. (called the *evening*), six hours after midnight when the morning began extending 6 P.M. (called morning), closing one complete 24 hour day. This method makes it easier to get the total. See Figure 1

Figure 1 Cycle of a Day

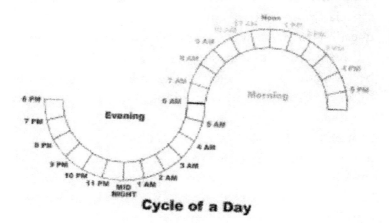

Cycle of a Day

The evening lasted 12 hours and the morning lasted 12 hours. Evening began at 6 P.M. and morning began at 6 A.M. We know Jesus knew this by looking at John 11:9- "Are there not twelve hours in the day?" So, we have established both how long one day is and when it begins and ends, according to the Bible from the beginning through the New Testament. The Jewish people still view their days the same way. There is no mistake about it. When read in context, the word for day *yom* is always apparent and consistent. When scholars say that a day means only part of a day they turn to Esther 4:16 as a prime example of argument. If they would only stop and count, the complete time clearly passes as it should by the fifth chapter and verse one. What are they afraid of?

Somewhere along the way modern man in his traditional wisdom changed our days to begin and end at midnight. Nevertheless, for the purpose of viewing God's truth, in this text, we will view the day and night as the Bible does instead of in the tradition of man. If we add the sum of three days and three nights we should come up with a total of 72 hours: 24 (hours in a day) times 3 (days), or 12 (hours) times 6 (evening and morning periods) each equals 72. Now traditionally, both the world and Christendom places the timetable of Christ in his tomb on Friday evening and raises Him on Sunday morning. Let's look at the time line:

Friday 6 PM till Saturday 6 PM till Sunday 6 AM
<--------24 hours--------> <-12 hours->

Now let's see. 24 + 12 = 36 hours. That's only half the time required to fulfill the prophecy. Jesus came to fulfill prophecy. Very eye opening! One half the time needed to show authenticity. Only 36 hours would be a false sign by Matthew 12:40 standards, now wouldn't it? Yet, even though Jesus rested his Messiahship and our eternities on this one sign, it doesn't seem to even register to the scholars. Why? Is now the time for this awakening, at the still dawning of the 3rd millennium?

CHAPTER 6

SO AS JONAH

Certainly we should shun the traditions of men in opposition to the word of God! Is it any doubt that Satan wants mankind to think that the story of Jonah and the whale was a myth? It is because Christ's Messiahship rests on Jonah and those truths. Jesus wouldn't have used a fictional account to give credence to such a critical time. Now man traditionally has said this great fish was a whale. Not necessarily so. Exact translations render it sea-monster or great fish. For all intents and purposes it was a special fish created by God for just this occasion. This also does not exclude a dinosauric fish. From the book of Job 40:15 - 41:34, God speaks of two creatures in the present tense: Behemoth and Leviathan, that are present after the flood. They have distinct as well as probably extinct dinosauric properties. Discoveries located at the Creation Evidence Museum in Glen Rose, Texas show fossil proof that dinosaurs lived contemporaneously with man. It was truly amazing to go there as I did in the summer of 1997 to see for myself. I saw with my own eyes the human fossilized indentations of human feet inside a dinosaur footprint, both beneath and preserved underwater. Mankind is still finding more different kinds of creatures beneath the oceans depths and in the forests deep. Future discoveries may be staggering and unfathomable.

Let's turn to Jonah 1:17- "Now the Lord had prepared a great fish to swallow up Jonah. And Jonah was in the belly of the fish three days and three nights." But remember, the devil knows that the belief and adherence to Good Friday will keep Jesus as the Messiah away from His glorified place in a lot of people's minds! Good for Satan maybe. Jonah was entombed (Jonah 2:2) 72 hours (Jonah 1:17) and then was resurrected by God through the process of the fish vomiting him up (Jonah 2:10) and became a type of savior to the people of Nineveh by warning them. Also, Jesus would stay 72 hours entombed and then be the resurrected God, Savior of the world. Jesus rose the *third* day. Several scriptures say this. Genesis 1:13 also states "And there was evening and there was morning, a third day takes into account the entire *completion* of the third 24 hours period, not happening before or during. The suspense builds! (Acts 17:30; Ephesians 4:18), we should not be guilty of the warning found in Mark 7:13- "Making the word of God of none effect through your tradition, which ye have delivered: and many such like things do ye".

Notice Mark 8:31- "And He began to teach them, that the Son of Man must suffer many things, and be rejected of the elders, and of the chief priests, and scribes, and be killed, and after three days rise again." If Jesus was crucified on Friday, one day after would be Saturday evening, two days after would have been Sunday evening, and three days after the resurrection would have occurred Monday evening. A Sunday morning resurrection would have been in the middle of the second day. Keep this in mind.

I am not insinuating that Jesus is an imposter. I am stating though plainly that we have been led astray as to the truth of what the Bible simply says on this important subject. Let's listen to and believe what Jesus has told us. Jesus was not crucified on Good Friday, nor did He arise Sunday morning at or anywhere near sunrise. This was not a "sun rise" (pagan origin) Sunday morning but a very important "Son rise" at the correct time, early on the first day of the week. We have listened with itching ears (2 Timothy 4:3) for much too long. Now let's see if we can examine these and other supporting and clarifying verses placing all the puzzle pieces together (2 Timothy 2:15) to complete the unity that has been here all along for us to bring out into place, instead of allowing the hierarchy to do our thinking for us. If they have been this wrong on this subject just think at the possibilities of them being wrong on a myriad of others. Let's continue.

Jesus died at about the ninth hour (3 P.M.). See Matthew 27:46-50. Each day of the daytime 12 hours begins at sunrise. The first hour of the day is at 7 A.M. and so on, making noon the sixth hour. The preparation day of "a" Sabbath was about to dawn. Verse 57 states when it was evening, Joseph of Arimathea tried to get the body of Jesus into the tomb before sunset, which initiates the Sabbath. However, sunset precedes evening, and verse

57 says it was *evening* already. Therefore, by the time the stone was rolled against the entrance, it was definitely after the Sabbath started. It was also after preparation for Passover. This wasn't just a yearly Passover. This is the PASSOVER of ALL TIME. It wasn't just rolling sins up. This is for the sins of the whole world for all time: past, present, and far into the future. This Joseph, it says, was rich. He already had a tomb prepared for himself in which to place the body of Jesus. Now, you can try all you want and come with legal precedence and customs and traditions to place him in the tomb before the Sabbath but evening had already come. Golgotha was on the northwest side of Jerusalem. The dead were not embalmed or cremated so care had to be taken to not allow animals to get to the bodies. Because of the prevailing west wind and the smell of the decaying bodies, it was not customary to bury the dead on the western side of the city or temple. A rich man such as Joseph would have had a prime location perhaps close but definitely not directly on the westside. The burial site was ready for occupancy. Remember the time of day it is because 72 hours after Jesus is placed in the heart of the earth, the sepulcher, it would be in three days at the same time of day. This timing is most critical. If it was before sunset then we would have a Sabbath resurrection and no reason for the first day of the week to have its significance. Now, here would be the best place to put this next verse for our study. However, it could be placed in several for us to see its importance.

There is one denomination I am aware of that holds to the 7th day resurrection wholeheartedly. But it is clear by reading verse 57 that it was already *evening* (after sunset) when Joseph of Arimathea came and asked for the body of Jesus. It was the Jewish custom according to law to bury the dead before the Sabbath began at sunset, since no work was to be done on the Sabbath. But with everything that happened after sunset per John 19:36, Nicodemus had brought about a hundred pounds of myrrh and aloes. This mixture was wound in the linen clothes prior to burial. All this took precious time. Using a lot of spices was customary. Josephus, a very early historian, recorded the carrying of the body of Herod followed by five hundred servants and freedmen carrying sweet spices.

Remember, Jesus is still Lord of the Sabbath (Matthew 12:8, Luke 6:5). We know that Jesus was crucified on a day prior to the Sabbath.

Of course, all of these verses are important but I would like to make special note of these two, Matt 27: 63 and 64. There are two forces at work here, one is proving his Messiahship by this authentication where he is accused as being that deceiver that said while he was still alive: "AFTER THREE DAYS I WILL ARISE AGAIN." Then the other solemnly assuring that no one would come and steal the corpse and make an even greater problem by commanding the sepulcher be made completely secure until the third day. Then they sealed the stone and the 72 critical hours begin. Some will want to start the clock after he was entombed but before the stone was rolled into place. No matter, the sun had already set. Even/evening had come when Joseph of Arimathea first showed up for Jesus' body. It is fitting that the Passover had just begun as well. He will arise after the second Sabbath, early on the first day of the week.

Picture donated by: John Logan

We also know He was resurrected after the Sabbath. But these two Sabbaths were not one and the same.

CHAPTER 7

AN HIGH DAY= FEAST DAY=SABBATH

Are all Sabbaths on Saturday? Is a Sabbath always the 7th day of the week? We know that a Sabbath day followed the crucifixion, but was it Saturday the day after Good Friday? God did rest on the Sabbath and it was the seventh day of the week. Were there other Sabbaths that were observed during that time period? Let's notice what John 19:14,31 says- "for that Sabbath day was an high day" or a sacred occasion. A "high day" or a feast day to the Jewish religion or Judiasm is an actual Sabbath. It does not need to be the 7th day or a Saturday. The Israelites observe several of these every year and each one is called a Sabbath. These Sabbaths can fall on any day of the week. In 1996 Passover was on a Thursday, in 1997 a Tuesday, in 1998 a Saturday, and in 1999 a Thursday. See Leviticus 16:29-31, 23:23-44.

Leviticus 23 begins telling us God's definition of a Sabbath. It includes every seventh day as we know as Saturday beginning at sunset Friday. The seventh day is in verse 3. And the feast of the Passover (15 of Abib, the 1st day of the Feast of Unleavened Bread to the Lord) is also a Sabbath, a holy convocation also referred to through verse 7. Upon looking up the Hebrew words that translated Sabbath, we find in these instances: *shabbath*, pronounced shab-bawth'. It means specifically the Sabbath, or every Sabbath. The Greek word *Sabbaton* has the same meaning as the Hebrew word *Shabbath* and can also be plural as in Sabbaths. On page 679 of the book I referenced "The Word Study Concordance" mid-page is the Greek word numbered 4521 and the following words are marked with a 3. But in Matthew 28:1 and in Mark 16:1 it is the second Sabbath that is being referred to. There is no getting around or circumventing Biblical text. I have spoken with some synagogues and they tell me that the only Sabbath is the seventh day, the day before the first day of the week. Well, that is not in agreement with their own books. Notwithstanding, all Christian Bibles and even the Tanakh include the books of Exodus, Numbers, Leviticus, and Isaiah.

Matthew 26:2- "You know that after two days the Passover is coming, And the Son of Man is to be delivered up for crucifixion." Here, we find that Jesus was crucified on the preparation of the Passover. This preparation day was Wednesday followed at 6 P.M. by the feast day (an annual Sabbath) which lasted until 6 P.M. or sunset Thursday. The Passover was Thursday as it was in 1999. See the 12th chapter of Exodus. I Corinthians 5:7- "For even Christ our Passover is sacrificed for us." See Number 28: 16-17. Jesus is a type of lamb: see Revelation 7:14

""And 12:11- "the blood of the Lamb" in this instance. See Gen 22:8, Isa 53:7, John 1:29, Acts 8:32, I Pet 1:19. There were 2 separate Sabbaths the week of Jesus' crucifixion. The 10th of Abib (Nisan) traditionally fell on a Sabbath (7th day of the week). A day called "an high day" or "holy convocation" or sacred occasion" was Thursday the 15th of Abib, with the 2nd Sabbath of the week coming beginning sunset Friday. With 2 separate Sabbaths that week, and with Christ laid in the tomb shortly after sunset Wednesday, and we count Three days and three nights (72 hours total), we have the following timeline:

Figure 2 3 Days And 3 Nights Timeline

M= Midnight
6= 6th hour (noon), darkness
N= Noon
9= 9th hour (3 P.M.)
L= Last Supper
J= Joseph of Arimathea
    came for Jesus' body
G= Garden of Gethsemane
B= Burial in the Tomb, heart of the earth
T= Arrest and subsequent Trial
A= Arose after 72 hours
C= Crucifixion
S= Sunday morning, came to the Tomb

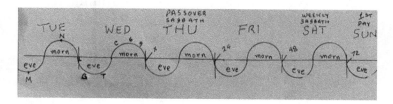

Figure 11

Mark 16:9-- "Now when Jesus was risen early the first day of the week," proves that Jesus rose *early* on the first day of the week, shortly after sunset; this was after the second Sabbath. He did not arise *late* on the first day of the week. A 6 A.M. sunrise would be half the day gone for the first day of the week. Remember when worshipers assemble on Sunday morning at 10 A.M. the first day of the week, it is in the last half of the day, 16 hours old, two thirds of the day is gone.

It was a first day of the week resurrection, not a Sunday morning resurrection as we happen to count days today beginning at midnight. No one (human) *saw* Christ arise. The witnesses came on Sunday morning to the tomb, while it was yet dark, as the sun was beginning to rise, at dawn (Mark 16:6; Luke 24:1; John 20:1). Notice that Jesus was not there! Notice how the angel says "He is not here, but is risen" (Mark 16:6; Luke 24:6; Matt 28:5,6).

Christ authenticated the absolute! See I Cor 15:3,4. His death, burial, and resurrection were per the Scriptures, not opposing them. Even in Daniel's 70 weeks concerning the Messiah (Dan. 9:24-27), Jesus was to be cut off in the midst (middle) of the week. The middle of the week counting from 6 P.M. Saturday to the next is Wednesday at 6 A.M. during the arrest and trial which is the *cut off* point.

Some always mistakenly equate darkness or nighttime with evil. There are times this is so but each one should be taken in context. There are scores of examples in the

Bible that do not support this theory, one of which is Psalms 134:1- "Behold, bless ye the Lord, all ye servants of the Lord, which by night stand in the house of the Lord." He is Lord of the night as well as the day, each and every moment.

Also note Luke 23:56 and Mark 16:1. Mary Magdalene and her companions did not buy and prepare their spices to anoint the body of Jesus until after the Sabbath was over. They could not purchase or prepare them until after the (first) Sabbath (Thursday), yet after preparing the spices (on Friday) they rested the (second) Sabbath day (Saturday) according to the commandment. Is it any wonder then that we need to study to show ourselves approved unto God. The texts we've just seen proves there were two Sabbaths that week with a day in between, otherwise we find contradictions and missing pieces in the 36-hour theory. The only true contradictions to be found are in the traditions and commandments and philosophies and the empty deceptions of men and the world, and not after Christ (Colossians 2:8). Mark 7:7- "Howbeit in vain do they worship me, teaching for doctrines the commandments of men."

CHAPTER 8

CHRISTIANS ASSEMBLE BY EXAMPLE AND TO COMMEMORATE

If we as Christians are going by Biblical example, then why not assemble as the early church did *early* on the first day of the week according to God, not according to our history or ancestry? That special time is sacred. And it is the example set before us. Why have we allowed the devil to have his due? Why have we given Satan the rule over Saturday evening and night? Of course, Sunday morning is still the first day of the week, but our Sunday evening services after sunset are not. Let's see if the Bible gives us any clues as to when the best time should be for Christians to assemble. The examples I see are in the New Testament. One of the things that takes place is the breaking of bread accompanied with communion in remembrance of Christ's death, burial and resurrection but the important thing is the time set aside for this memorial. The time is a weekly time set as close as possible to the day and time of His resurrection. Let's look at John 20:

19- "Then the same day at evening, being the first day of the week, when the doors were shut where the disciples were assembled for fear of the Jews, came Jesus and stood in the midst, and saith unto them. PEACE BE UNTO YOU." This same day according to this verse is none other than the first day of the week. But it is evening. So, it would be Saturday evening, close to resurrection time, and not Sunday evening 24 hours away. In Mark 16: 9 we find .... "Jesus was risen early the first day of the week,..." In the same context we see that the first day of the week begins shortly after sunset -- still Saturday evening from our point of view. Most, but not all, church services happen Sunday mornings. If we used 10 A.M. as a norm then that would be 16 hours after the first day of the week began, which would be late in the day not early. Two-thirds of the day is gone. Even with a service beginning at 6 A.M. Sunday morning, the day is already half gone. The example set before us to follow is a far cry from the inconvenience we give to it.

Acts 20:7 has always been described to me as Paul preaching a very long-winded sermon beginning Sunday morning and continuing until midnight. It was told to me that the saints assembled like we do now according to scriptural example. If the church assembled at approximately 10 A.M. and sang songs of praise and prayed and had communion, then it was probably around 11 A.M. when Paul began his sermon. If he preached until midnight it would have lasted over twelve hours. I blindly accepted this interpretation until I took the time to read through verses 11 and 8. Read through it yourself and see what you think. We can have either one of the following two scenarios, but not both. Which one makes the most sense to you?

If Paul preached to them at around 10 A.M. on Sunday morning, he would have had a very long sermon, over twelve hours to preach until midnight. The lights mentioned in verse 8 wouldn't have been needed for most of that time. Plus, after 6 P.M. Sunday evening wouldn't have even been the first day of the week anymore. This midnight would also have been on the second day of the week. His departure would have been Monday morning.

If Paul preached to them beginning the worship service shortly after 6 P.M. Saturday evening, *early* on the first day of the week, then he had around a 5-hour sermon (still a long sermon). Verse 8 tells us that it was dark enough to have lights during this time. Morrow means morning, so he had departed on Sunday morning.

To me, scenario #2 makes the most sense, especially in light of and in the context of knowing when Jesus, our Lord and Savior, arose. The point is that this is the scripture that most use to prove a Sunday-morning-first-day-of-the-week-church-service example. However, it doesn't prove that at all. Since Christ rose early on the first day of the week which was shortly after sunset Saturday night, this example scripture proves that even better.

Christ's authenticity of Messiahship has been proven maybe for the first time in history (*His story*). He was in the sepulcher no shorter than 72 hours. He was not buried before sunset Wednesday. Thursday was the Passover, a Sabbath, an High Day, A Holy Convocation. Friday

-- they prepared the spices and ointments. After the preparation, they rested on the Sabbath day, Saturday. Shortly after sunset, Jesus arose, after three days and three nights, demonstrating He is God. Sunday morning, about half of the first day of the week was gone, they came to an empty tomb. HE IS RISEN!

Mark 16:2-7

"And very early in the morning the first day of the week, they came unto the sepulcher at the rising of the sun. And they said among themselves, Who shall roll us away the stone from the door of the sepulcher? And when they looked, they saw that the stone was rolled away: for it was very great. And entering into the sepulcher, they saw a young man (Matthew says angel) sitting on the right side, clothed in a long white garment; and they were affrighted. And he saith unto them, Be not affrighted: "Ye seek Jesus of Nazareth, which was crucified: he is risen; he is not here: behold the place where they laid him. But g**o your way, tell his disciples and Peter that he goeth before you into Galilee: there shall ye see him, as he said unto you.**"

IN CONCLUSION

Several similar 72-hour conclusions, as well as other 36-hour ones trying to fit the mold, have been attempted, but each has fallen short. Here, not only do all the pieces fit, but they are also proven with your own Bible. Sunday is an important day for each of us. It is, after all, the first day of the week and most believe that Christ arose Sunday morning. We call it the Lord's day and those that respect and believe attend a place that remembers and shows they have an appropriate response. Why? Because the time he was resurrected, either through our consciousness or our subconscious, has value and importance to our lives. He fulfilled every prophecy and as a result, we hold dear a host of songs that touch us in some way, like "Amazing Grace" or the invitation song when I was baptized, "Oh Why Not Tonight". And regardless of the importance we give it, we behave in a way that shows we do a lot by example and not by repetitiveness or habit or indoctrination. So, the time of resurrection is both crucial and critical whether it is from Jesus' or our perspective. Will knowing the truth from where we found it make a difference? I pray it will. Time will tell. It took 2,000 years to get us here and I don't think we are in any form of the dark ages or at least we shouldn't be. There is no doubt that Jesus did what he was sent here to do. We have followed our religious leaders for so long, but what if we were given a break, like a pandemic, to give us time to reflect and maybe tweak our direction? If they have been wrong or misleading about this major detail, what other discoveries are waiting to be made since we now have more time to read and study and reflect and pray? So, if we picked a time to assemble as Christians on the first day of the week, when would it be? A viable option would be right after sunset closing the Sabbath, correspondingly would be right after sunset Saturday evening the same time. Both would be early on the first day of the week. Of course this would encroach upon Satan's and his minions' favorite playtime.

Thank you for taking this critical 72 hour countdown after the CROSS.

BIBLIOGRAPHY

Gardner, Joseph, ed. *Reader's Digest Atlas of the Bible*. Pleasantville, NY: Reader's Digest Association, Inc., 1981.

Martin William. *The Layman's Bible Encyclopedia*. Chicago, IL: The Lakeside Press 1964.

Strong, James. *The New Strong's Concordance of the Bible*, Popular Edition. Nashville, TN: Thomas Nelson Publishers. 1985.

Unger, Merrill. *Unger's Bible Dictionary*. Chicago, IL: Moody Press, 1985.

Ward, Kaari, ed. Jesus and *His Times*. Pleasantville, NY: Reader's Digest Association, Inc., 1987.

Whiston, William. *Josephus Complete Work*. Grand Rapids, MI: Kregel Publications,1960.

Wright, John, Ed. "Calendar of the Year", "Science and Technology". *The Universal Almanac 1993*. Kansas City, MO: Andrews and McMeel, 1992.

Young, Robert. *Analytical Concordance to the Bible*. Grand Rapids, MI: William B. Eerdmans Publishing Company, 1970.

Ford, Kelly Don "Ancient Signs of Deception." Duncanville, TX 1999